NFL TEAMS

BY LARRY MACK

THE CAROLINA PANTHERS STORY

BELLWETHER MEDIA · MINNEAPOLIS, MN

Are you ready to take it to the extreme? Torque books thrust you into the action-packed world of sports, vehicles, mystery, and adventure. These books may include dirt, smoke, fire, and chilling tales. **WARNING**: read at your own risk.

This edition first published in 2017 by Bellwether Media, Inc.

Library of Congress Cataloging-in-Publication Data

Names: Mack, Larry.
Title: The Carolina Panthers Story / by Larry Mack.
Description: Minneapolis, MN : Bellwether Media, Inc., 2017. | Series: Torque: NFL Teams | Includes bibliographical references and index. | Audience: Ages: 7-12. | Audience: Grades: 3 through 7.
Identifiers: LCCN 2016002571 | ISBN 9781626173590 (hardcover : alk. paper)
Subjects: LCSH: Carolina Panthers (Football team)–History–Juvenile literature.
Classification: LCC GV956.C27 M33 2017 | DDC 796.332/640975676–dc23
LC record available at http://lccn.loc.gov/2016002571

Printed in the United States of America, North Mankato, MN.

TABLE OF CONTENTS

CONFERENCE CHAMPIONS

The Carolina Panthers line up against the Arizona Cardinals on January 24, 2016. It is the National Football **Conference** (NFC) Championship game.

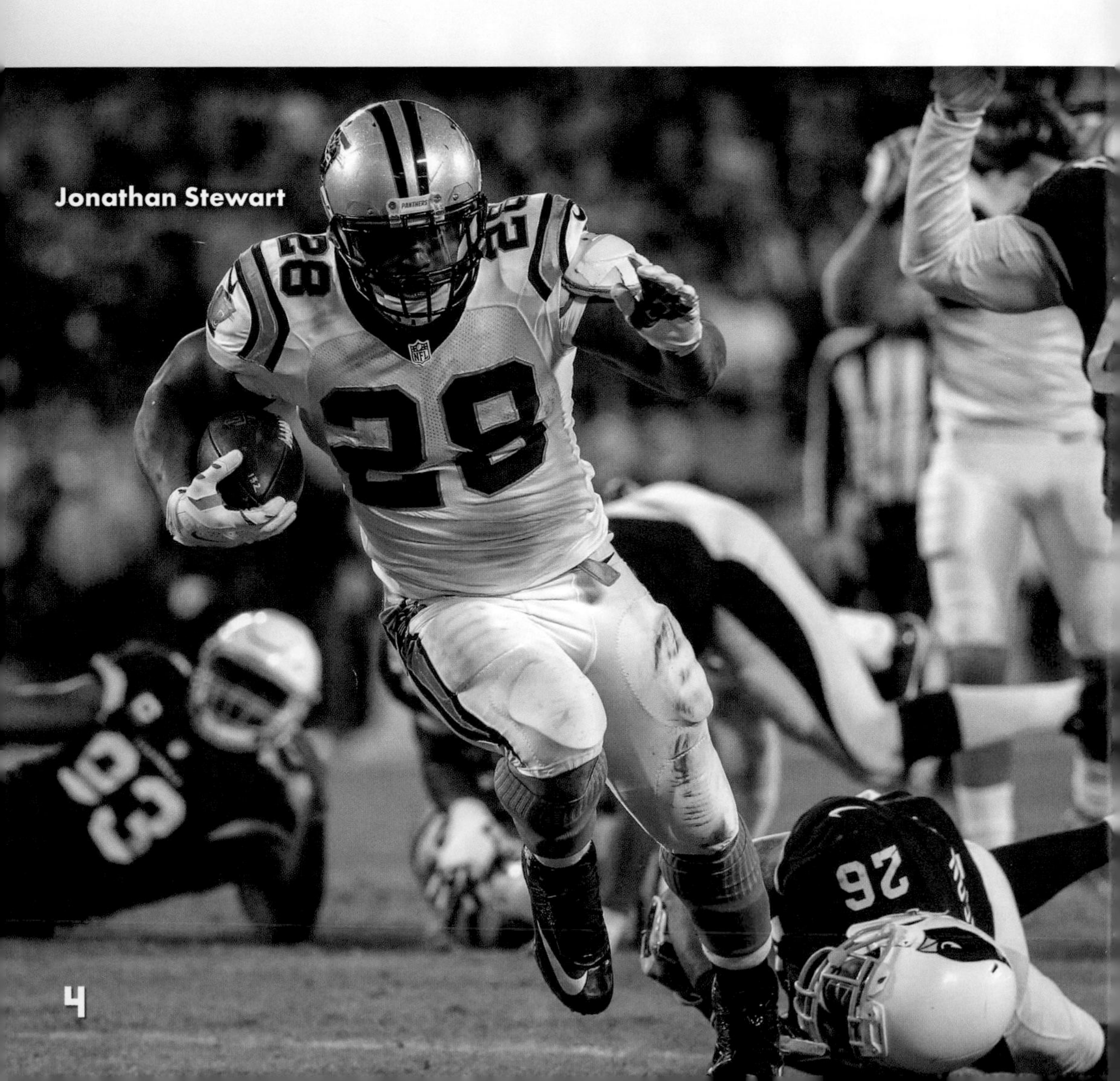

Jonathan Stewart

Ted Ginn, Jr.

The Panthers quickly pull ahead with a field goal and two touchdowns. The Cardinals cannot keep up. At halftime, the Panthers are ahead by 17.

Cam Newton

In the third quarter, Carolina **quarterback** Cam Newton gets the ball. He runs to the right. Then he heads for the goal line. He leaps high into the end zone. Another touchdown!

Finally, the clock runs out. The score is 49 to 15. The Panthers are headed to **Super Bowl** 50!

SCORING TERMS

END ZONE

the area at each end of a football field; a team scores by entering the opponent's end zone with the football.

EXTRA POINT

a score that occurs when a kicker kicks the ball between the opponent's goal posts after a touchdown is scored; 1 point.

FIELD GOAL

a score that occurs when a kicker kicks the ball between the opponent's goal posts; 3 points.

SAFETY

a score that occurs when a player on offense is tackled behind his own goal line; 2 points for defense.

TOUCHDOWN

a score that occurs when a team crosses into its opponent's end zone with the football; 6 points.

TWO-POINT CONVERSION

a score that occurs when a team crosses into its opponent's end zone with the football after scoring a touchdown; 2 points.

BIG WINS, GREAT TRADITIONS

The Carolina Panthers were the 29th team to join the National Football League (NFL). Smart coaches and hardworking players have led the team to win big games.

VICTORY SONG

The song "Sweet Caroline" is part of a team tradition. It plays over stadium speakers after home victories. Fans sing along to celebrate!

The Panthers have many fun cheers and game traditions for the players and fans. These make the fans feel connected to their team.

North Carolina and South Carolina are both represented by the Panthers. The team plays home games at Bank of America Stadium in Charlotte, North Carolina. Fans call the stadium "The **Vault**" because it is named after a bank.

BIG BRONZE CATS

Six huge panthers sit outside Bank of America Stadium. They are made of bronze metal. They are the largest bronze statues ever made in the United States.

The Panthers play in the NFC South **Division**. This division was created in 2002.

The NFC South includes the Atlanta Falcons, New Orleans Saints, and Tampa Bay Buccaneers. These teams have become great **rivals**.

NFL DIVISIONS

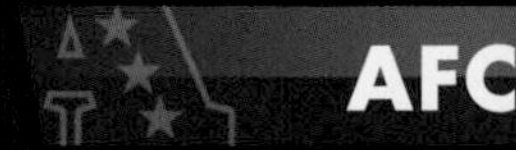

AFC NORTH

BALTIMORE **RAVENS**

CINCINNATI **BENGALS**

CLEVELAND **BROWNS**

PITTSBURGH **STEELERS**

AFC EAST

BUFFALO **BILLS**

MIAMI **DOLPHINS**

PATRIOTS

NEW YORK **JETS**

AFC SOUTH

TEXANS

INDIANAPOLIS **COLTS**

JACKSONVILLE **JAGUARS**

TENNESSEE **TITANS**

AFC WEST

DENVER **BRONCOS**

CHIEFS

OAKLAND **RAIDERS**

SAN DIEGO **CHARGERS**

NFC

NFC NORTH

CHICAGO
BEARS

DETROIT
LIONS

GREEN BAY
PACKERS

MINNESOTA
VIKINGS

NFC EAST

DALLAS
COWBOYS

GIANTS

PHILADELPHIA
EAGLES

WASHINGTON
REDSKINS

NFC SOUTH

FALCONS

CAROLINA
PANTHERS

NEW ORLEANS
SAINTS

BUCCANEERS

NFC WEST

CARDINALS

LOS ANGELES
RAMS

SAN FRANCISCO
49ERS

SEATTLE
SEAHAWKS

THEN TO NOW

In 1995, the Carolina Panthers were an NFL **expansion team**. They enjoyed early success. The Panthers became division champions in their second season. In 2004, the Panthers went all the way to Super Bowl 38!

But the team and their fans have had rough seasons, too. In 2010, they lost 14 out of 16 games.

1995 season

SUPER BOWL 38
FEBRUARY 1, 2004

In 2011, the Panthers **drafted** quarterback Cam Newton. They also hired Ron Rivera to be their head coach.

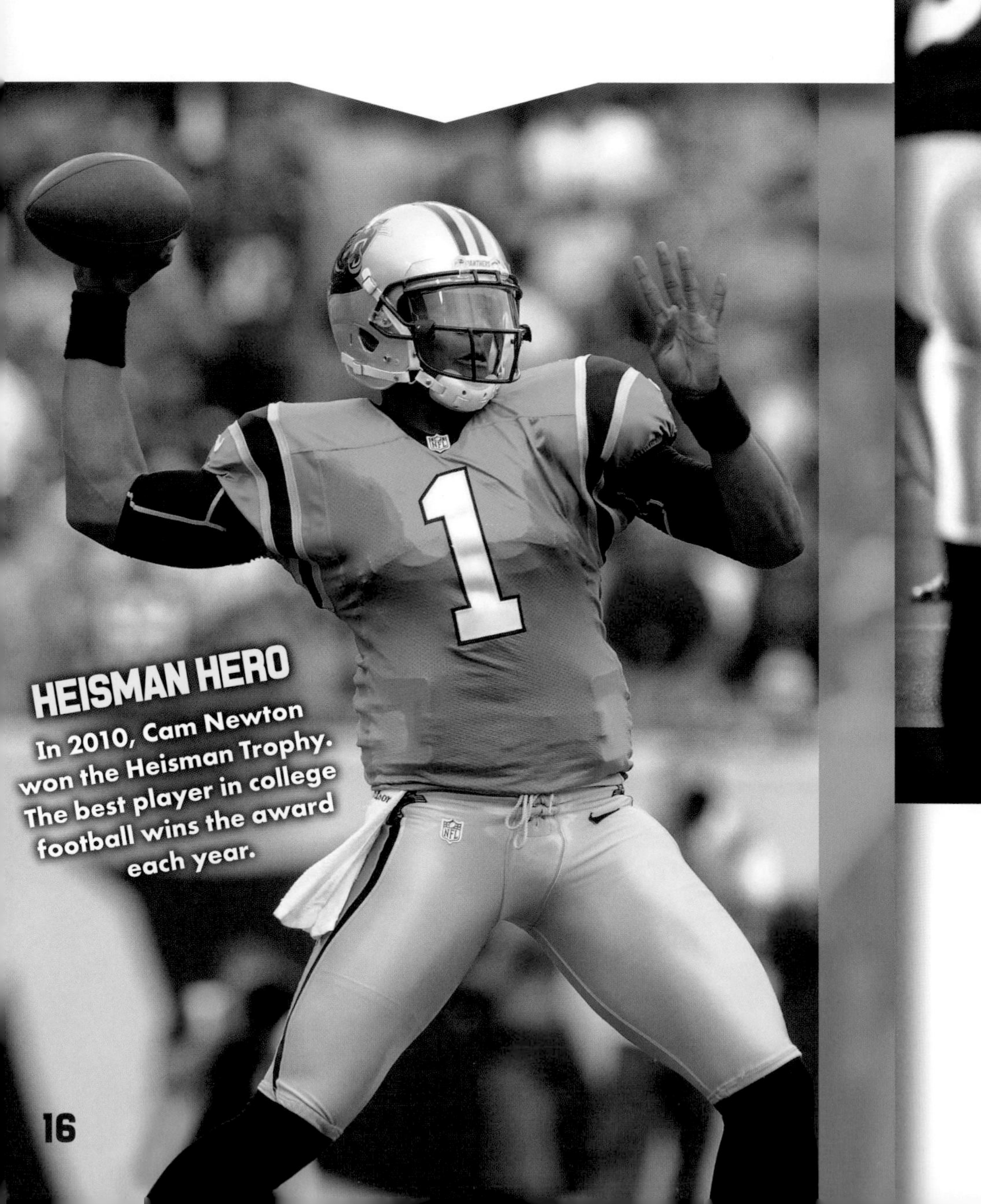

HEISMAN HERO

In 2010, Cam Newton won the Heisman Trophy. The best player in college football wins the award each year.

Ron Rivera

Coach Rivera was named the NFL Coach of the Year for 2013 and 2015. Together, he and Newton led the Panthers to Super Bowl 50.

PANTHERS TIMELINE

1993

Approved as an NFL expansion team for North Carolina

1995

Played first-ever game, beating the Jacksonville Jaguars (20-14)

1996

Played first game at Bank of America Stadium

1996

Won NFC West title

1997

Won first-ever playoff game, beating the Dallas Cowboys (26-17)

2002

Moved to the NFC South Division

2004

Won the NFC Championship, beating the Philadelphia Eagles

14 FINAL SCORE **3**

2016

Set record for most points in an NFC Championship game, beating the Arizona Cardinals

49 FINAL SCORE **15**

2011

Drafted quarterback Cam Newton

2015

Won third straight NFC South title

2016

Celebrated Cam Newton's 2015 NFL awards for Offensive Player of the Year and Most Valuable Player (MVP)

Linebacker Sam Mills was the Panthers' first superstar. He did not miss a single game. After Mills **retired**, he was an assistant coach for the Panthers. He stayed with the team until cancer took him in 2005.

Sam Mills as assistant coach

LIKE FATHER, LIKE SON

Sam Mills' son became an assistant coach for the Panthers in 2006. His name is Sam Mills III.

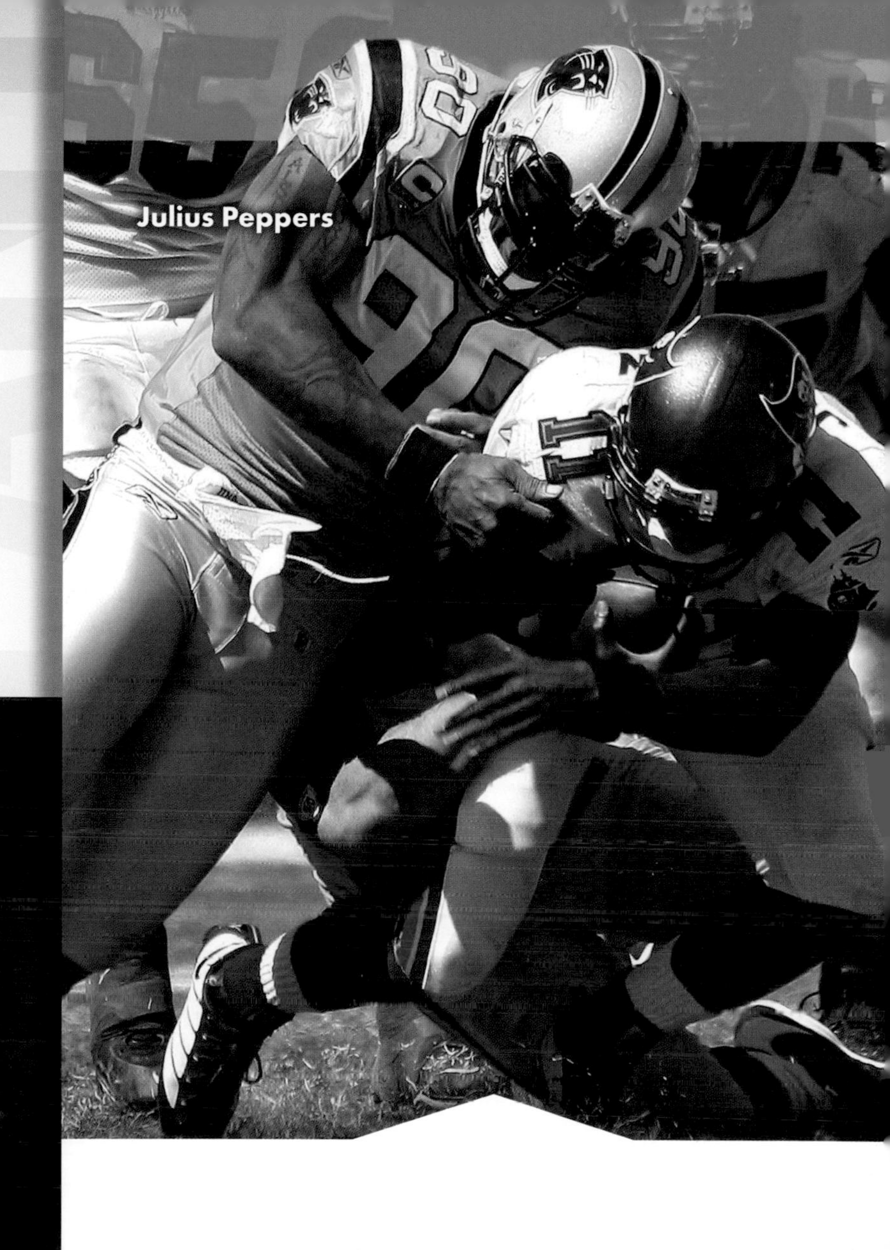

Julius Peppers

Another top Carolina player was Julius Peppers. The **defensive end** set a team record for most **sacks**. He made 81 from 2002 to 2009.

The Panthers have had tough players on **offense** over the years. Quarterback Jake Delhomme threw many touchdown passes to **wide receiver** Steve Smith. He also handed the ball off to DeAngelo Williams.

Today's top Carolina star is Cam Newton. The young quarterback is tall, strong, and fast.

TEAM GREATS

SAM MILLS
LINEBACKER AND COACH
1995–2004

STEVE SMITH
WIDE RECEIVER
2001–2013

JULIUS PEPPERS
DEFENSIVE END
2002–2009

Steve Smith

JAKE DELHOMME
QUARTERBACK
2003–2009

DEANGELO WILLIAMS
RUNNING BACK
2006–2014

CAM NEWTON
QUARTERBACK
2011–PRESENT

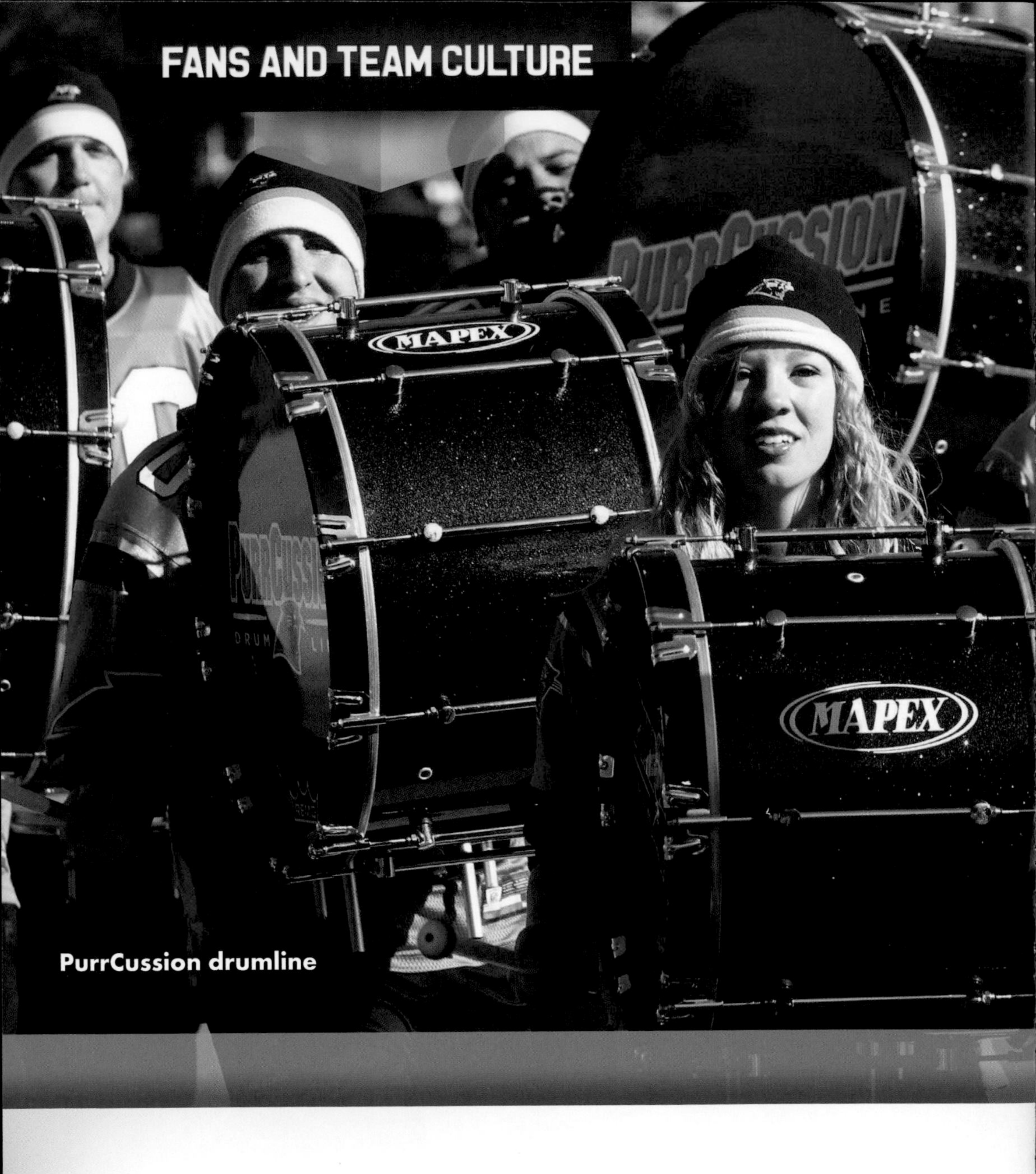

PurrCussion drumline

The Panthers are one of the newer NFL teams. But they have formed great traditions already. The PurrCussion **drumline** entertains fans. It also helps introduce players before games.

Team mascot, Sir Purr, and the Black and Blue Crew pump up the crowd!

Sir Purr

An inspiring team tradition is the "Keep Pounding" drum **ceremony**. Before each home game, fans stand up together. Then a drummer strikes a huge drum four times. The crowd cheers and the game begins.

"Keep pounding" was something Coach Mills had always told his players. This encouraged them to play hard. His words still motivate the Panthers today!

MORE ABOUT THE PANTHERS

Team name:
Carolina Panthers

Team name explained:
Named after wildcats that are powerful, fast, and strong

Joined NFL: 1995

Conference: NFC

Division: South

Main rivals: Atlanta Falcons, New Orleans Saints

Hometown: Charlotte, North Carolina

Training camp location: Wofford College, Spartanburg, South Carolina

THE CAROLINAS

N
W E
S

Home stadium name: Bank of America Stadium

Stadium opened: 1996

Seats in stadium: 75,412

Logo: A black cat outlined in blue, with silver fangs and eyes

Colors: Black, blue, silver, white

Mascot: Sir Purr

GLOSSARY

ceremony—an event that marks an important occasion

conference—a large grouping of sports teams that often play one another

defensive end—a player on defense whose job is to tackle the player with the ball

division—a small grouping of sports teams that often play one another; usually there are several divisions of teams in a conference.

drafted—chose a college athlete to play for a professional team

drumline—a group of musicians who play drums and cymbals, usually to pump up a crowd

expansion team—a new team added to a sports league

linebacker—a player on defense whose main job is to make tackles and stop passes; a linebacker stands just behind the defensive linemen.

offense—the group of players who try to move down the field and score

quarterback—a player on offense whose main job is to throw and hand off the ball

retired—ended a career

rivals—teams that are long-standing opponents

sacks—plays during which a player on defense tackles the opposing quarterback for a loss of yards

Super Bowl—the championship game for the NFL

vault—a room for keeping valuables safe

wide receiver—a player on offense whose main job is to catch passes from the quarterback

TO LEARN MORE

AT THE LIBRARY

Frisch, Nate. *The Story of the Carolina Panthers.* Mankato, Minn.: Creative Education, 2013.

Monnig, Alex. *Carolina Panthers.* Mankato, Minn.: Child's World, 2015.

Teitelbaum, Michael. *NFC South.* Mankato, Minn.: Child's World, 2012.

ON THE WEB

Learning more about the Carolina Panthers is as easy as 1, 2, 3.

1. Go to www.factsurfer.com.

2. Enter "Carolina Panthers" into the search box.

3. Click the "Surf" button and you will see a list of related web sites.

With factsurfer.com, finding more information is just a click away.

INDEX

The images in this book are reproduced through the courtesy of: Corbis, front cover (large, small), pp. 4-5, 5, 23 (right); Erik S. Lesser/ EPA/ Newscom, pp. 6-7, 7; David T. Foster III/ Charlotte Observer/ TNS/ Alamy, pp. 8-9; CLS Design, pp. 10-11; f11photo, p. 11; Margaret Bowles/ Cal Sport Media/ Alamy, pp. 12-13; Deposit Photos/ Glow Images, pp. 12-13 (logos), 18-19 (logos), 28-29 (logos); Al Golub/ AP Images, p. 14; Lionel Hahn/ KRT/ Newscom, p. 15; Scott A. Miller/ ZUMA Press/ Alamy, p. 16; Tribune Content Agency LLC/ Alamy, pp. 16-17, 19, 23 (middle), 26; Doug Mills/ AP Images, p. 18 (top); Bob Leverone/ KRT/ Newscom, p. 18 (bottom); David T. Foster III/ KRT/ Newscom, p. 19 (top); Chuck Burton/ AP Images, pp. 20-21; Margaret Bowles/ Southcreek Global/ ZUMA Press/ Alamy, pp. 21, 22-23, 22 (middle, right); George Gojkovich/ Getty Images, p. 22 (left); Evan Pinkus/ AP Images, p. 23; Bob Leverone/ AP Images, p. 24; Anthony Barham/ Southcreek Global/ ZUMA Press/ Alamy, p. 25; Kent Smith/ AP Images, pp. 26-27; Donald Page/ Southcreek Global/ ZUMA Press/ Alamy, p. 28; digidreamgrafix,